KUNSTLER

BY
JEFFREY SWEET

★

DRAMATISTS
PLAY SERVICE
INC.

NOTE ON BILLING

Anyone receiving permission to produce is required to give credit to the Author as sole and exclusive Author of the Play on the title page of all programs distributed in connection with performances of the Play and in all instances in which the title of the Play appears, including printed or digital materials for advertising, publicizing or otherwise exploiting the Play and/or a production thereof. Please see your production license for font size and typeface requirements.

Be advised that there may be additional credits required in all programs and promotional material. Such language will be listed under the "Additional Billing" section of production licenses. It is the licensee's responsibility to ensure any and all required billing is included in the requisite places, per the terms of the license.

SPECIAL NOTE ON SONGS/RECORDINGS

Dramatists Play Service neither holds the rights to nor grants permission to use any songs or recordings mentioned in the Play. Permission for performances of copyrighted songs, arrangements or recordings mentioned in this Play is not included in our license agreement. The permission of the copyright owner(s) must be obtained for any such use. For any songs and/or recordings mentioned in the Play, other songs, arrangements, or recordings may be substituted provided permission from the copyright owner(s) of such songs, arrangements or recordings is obtained; or songs, arrangements or recordings in the public domain may be substituted.

For William and Patricia Snyder

KUNSTLER premiered at Hudson Stage Company (Denise Bessette, Dan Foster, and Olivia Sklar, Artistic Producers) in the Woodward Hall Theatre of Pace University on April 26, 2013. It was directed by Annette O'Toole; the scenic design was by James J. Fenton; the costume design was by Leslie Bernstein; the lighting design was by Andrew Gmoser; and the production manager was Doug Ballard. The cast was as follows:

KUNSTLER .... Jeff McCarthy
KERRY .... Keona Welch

KUNSTLER was revived in a revised form produced by AND Theatre Company, as part of the New York Fringe Festival, on August 10, 2014. It was directed by Meagen Fay and the production stage manager was Kian Ross. The cast was as follows:

KUNSTLER .... Nick Wyman
KERRY .... Gillian Glasco

The Off-Broadway premiere of KUNSTLER was presented at 59E59 Theaters and produced by the Creative Place International (Patricia and William Snyder) in association with AND Theatre Company (Kristine Niven and Janice L. Goldberg, Artistic Directors), on February 17, 2017. It was directed by Meagen Fay, the set design was by James J. Fenton, the costume design was by Elivia Bovenzi, the lighting design was by Betsy Adams, the music and sound design was by Will Severin, and the production stage manager was Mary Jane Hansen. The cast was as follows:

KUNSTLER .... Jeff McCarthy
KERRY .... Nambi E. Kelley

This production transferred to Barrington Stage Company (Julianne Boyd, Artistic Director), Pittsfield, Massachusetts, on May 18, 2017. The cast was as follows:

KUNSTLER .... Jeff McCarthy
KERRY .... Erin Roché

CHARACTERS

WILLIAM KUNSTLER

KERRY NICHOLAS

KUNSTLER

A space suitable for a speaker in a university. It is up to the director to choose between, say, a lecture hall with an Ivy League feel or a more modern facility. Initially, the set should read realistically, but as the show progresses it should be able to accommodate different lighting to enhance the shifting moods of the piece.

Today the space is set up for a speaker—a podium upstage center and two chairs nearby.

At the start of the show, we hear—as if from outside the hall—the sound of fifteen or twenty demonstrators repeatedly chanting, "Kunstler is a traitor" and similar anti-Kunstler slogans. Lights come up into a "work light" feel. Trash is strewn across the floor, the two chairs are up-turned.

The sound of the chanting outside becomes louder as a door in the audience's section of the space opens, a door evidently leading to the outside where the demonstration is being held. Kerry, an African-American woman in her mid-twenties, enters. She is dressed in student-type attire (either skirt over opaque stockings—or 1995 slacks or jeans) chunky-heeled shoes, a shirt tied at the waist over camisole or body stocking top. She carries a backpack containing a light sweater (which she will switch out with the tied shirt) some notebooks, pen, etc... She turns and calls out...

KERRY. Keep it up. He loves the attention.

> *She closes the door and the demonstrators' chants recede. Now she sees the mess, mutters in irritation as she walks down to the stage.*

Oh come on! Real mature! *(Calling up to light booth.)* Jordan?!? Are you up there? Jordan? *(To herself.)* Damn it.

Realizing she is alone with this mess, she throws down her back-pack, and exits through a door leading to a hallway.

Maintenance? Hello? Is anybody here?

"Kunstler must go!" chants are interrupted by a demonstrator yelling, "That's him!" The crowd noise shifts into individual shouts overlapping—"Traitor!" "Hypocrite!" "Why are you defending rapists?" "Sellout!" "How much did Gotti pay you?" And then this gathers again into the chant of "Kunstler must go!" The sound increases as the door at the back of the house opens. Kunstler enters and, standing in the doorway, turns to them—

KUNSTLER. If you want to come in, we could talk about it. Have a conversation?

He evidently gets no takers and begins to make his way through the house toward the platform. He is wearing a gray summer-weight suit, off-white shirt—sleeves rolled up and with pen in his shirt pocket—and a tie. Under his arm Kunstler carries his suit jacket, a number of file folders filled with newspaper clippings, notes, pages of transcripts, etc. Each is wrapped with a rubber band. He also carries a yellow legal pad containing several pages of handwritten "Lawyer Jokes" and sections of a New York Times, *as well as a flyer from the demonstrators containing his picture with the word "traitor" stamped across it. Below his picture, the words, "William Kunstler is a sellout and a hypocrite. His defense of traitors, terrorists, and rapists is an insult to the causes for which he once stood. Boycott Kunstler and let the University know that you will not allow your tuition money to be paid to a man who no longer stands for Civil Rights! Or Justice!" The pamphlet should include typos and misspell-ings, to which Kunstler will refer later. In the right hand pocket of his slacks should be a neatly folded, white linen handkerchief. Kunstler steps through the garbage. Registering the upturned chairs, he crosses to them, rights them and sits in one with his back to the audience, putting his feet up on the other. He takes out the yellow legal pad and sits quietly, writing. Kerry reenters from audience door dragging a gray plastic trash can with the intention of putting the litter into it. She sees Kunstler.*

8

KERRY. Mr. Kunstler.

KUNSTLER. Hello—

KERRY. Mr. Kunstler, I'm Kerry Nicholas—

KUNSTLER. Kerry Nicholas, yes. Vice-chair of the program committee. My hosts!

KERRY. Yes, Matthew is—

KUNSTLER. Matthew is the committee chair and was supposed to be here.

KERRY. Yes, but—

KUNSTLER. He is currently on a train to Baltimore.

KERRY. Yes, family trouble. Matthew wanted me to tell you, he's very disappointed—

KUNSTLER. —he told me.

KERRY. He told you?

KUNSTLER. When he called me.

KERRY. He called you?

KUNSTLER. He tried to reach you.

KERRY. He did reach me. Actually, my answering machine. I just got it.

KUNSTLER. But he didn't reach you after he reached me to tell you he reached me.

KERRY. No.

KUNSTLER. But you'll soldier on despite your disappointment.

KERRY. My disappointment?

KUNSTLER. He happened to mention that—

KERRY. Oh?

KUNSTLER. —that you weren't in favor of inviting me.

KERRY. A number of distinguished people were proposed. It was put up to a vote.

KUNSTLER. That's democracy.

KERRY. We had a discussion, we had a vote—

KUNSTLER. And now you're stuck with me.

Chanting outside shifts to, "Kunstler is a self-hating Jew."

KERRY. That's overstating it. We're honored to have you here. And your visit has excited a lot of interest.

KUNSTLER. So I hear.

Kerry begins to stuff the trash into the trash can.

KERRY. We usually have a hospitality table. Fruit, crackers… If you'd like me to—

KUNSTLER. Just water will be fine.

At the mention of water, Kerry starts to exit off to get it. She turns back to him.

KERRY. I don't want you to think—

KUNSTLER. I don't. Relax.

KERRY. I'm going to be introducing you. I was wondering if there were anything in particular you'd like me to say.

KUNSTLER. You might get a few ideas from the protesters outside. The signs. Might give it a certain snap, don't you think? "I'm happy to present that notorious traitor and hypocrite…"

KERRY. I'm sorry about that.

KUNSTLER. No, sounds like that on a campus in 1995? It's refreshing. Or were you planning on being out there?

KERRY. Why don't I just—

Kerry exits off to get water and glass. Kunstler calls off to her.

KUNSTLER. Must say you get a better grade of insult from the newspapers. "The lawyer for causes of which none is more unpopular than he." That was in the *Washington Post*. And someone in the *New York Times* called me "a *schlemiel* with an edge." That one kind of hurt.

Kerry reenters with water pitcher and glass, which she places on the shelf inside the podium, then goes back to cleaning up the garbage on the floor and putting it in the bin.

KERRY. Oh?

KUNSTLER. You know what a *schlemiel* is?

KERRY. Not specifically.

KUNSTLER. A bumbler. Someone who habitually fucks things up.

KERRY. Ah.

KUNSTLER. I wrote a letter to them about that. That if they were going to call me names, they should come up with more accurate ones. Maybe a *chachem* or a *momser*.

KERRY. Don't know what those are either.

KUNSTLER. Then you probably shouldn't use them in the introduction. What kind of law?

KERRY. Excuse me?

KUNSTLER. You. What kind? Civil rights?

KERRY. Why, because I'm black?

KUNSTLER. No, you're right. I shouldn't assume.

KERRY. It's possible to be black and—

KUNSTLER. Of course, but something inspired you, made you want to do this. It's interesting to me what motivates people. You'd be surprised for how many people it's Atticus Finch. *To Kill a Mockingbird.* The book. Or Gregory Peck. Of course, you don't want to take that too far. Maybe you remember, he loses the case and his client is murdered. Generally speaking, that's not the outcome you want to go for.

KERRY. Winning is better.

KUNSTLER. The client kind of thinks so. It makes me happier, too.

KERRY. Well, it's for insights like this we invited you here.

> *She's finished clearing the garbage.*

KUNSTLER. So I take it that it wasn't Atticus Finch for you? I'm really asking you. I really want to know.

> *Kunstler starts to rise with difficulty. Kerry instinctively reaches to help him, but he waves her off.*

KERRY. Actually, I'm just introducing you.

KUNSTLER. I don't mean to press, if you're uncomfortable…

KERRY. It seems to me that would be a longer conversation, and we don't have the time.

> *He gathers his stuff as she pulls the chairs into a side-by-side position at an angle and downstage from the podium. He follows her.*

KUNSTLER. Perhaps later.

KERRY. The simple version, I guess, is that—this is going to be awfully general—

KUNSTLER. Understood.

KERRY. And not terribly original.

KUNSTLER. You have my permission not to be original.

KERRY. But whenever anything important happens, inevitably somewhere along the line it goes to law. Any change, any issue. See, I told you: very general.

KUNSTLER. No, I think what you're saying is—

KERRY. It's a way to be in the present. You know? To be part of the times. Part of the dialogue—

KUNSTLER. And you want to be part of the dialogue. You don't want to just read about it in the newspapers.

KERRY. No.

KUNSTLER. So—criminal law? Public interest? Copyright law? New technologies coming along, copyright law is going to be—Or you might try for, God forbid, being a judge. Not enough women—

KERRY. As I say, I haven't decided. Of course, I'll have student loans to pay off.

KUNSTLER. Sure, that will be a factor. Money is always a factor. But you don't want to let money take over, make all your choices for you.

KERRY. No, that wouldn't be good.

KUNSTLER. It can be a trap.

> *Lights flare up and down as if Jordan has arrived and is cueing up the board.*

KERRY. *(To the light booth.)* Oh great, you're here.

KUNSTLER. *(Continuing.)* Not that you don't know this. I'm sure you know this.

> *Kerry pushes the garbage bin offstage and returns.*

KERRY. *(To someone unseen in the house.)* I think we can open the doors now.

Kunstler puts on his jacket. The sound of the audience beginning to enter the space. In the background, we can still hear sounds of the demonstrators folding a few new taunts— "You're supporting a hypocrite." "He defends the Mafia and terrorists!" "Ask him why he defends rapists!" She nods to the chairs, and they sit. Kerry scribbles a few notes for her introduction. Kunstler nods in greeting to members of the audience as though they are just arriving. Kerry spots a friend in the audience, and, indicating Kunstler, mouths— "I'll tell you later." Kunstler turns to her, referencing the pad he's been writing on.

KUNSTLER. Listen: My birthday's coming up. The party's going to be at Caroline's—the comedy club?

KERRY. I'm sorry, what are we talking about?

KUNSTLER. My birthday party. At Caroline's.

KERRY. The comedy club.

KUNSTLER. It's on Broadway near, I think, Fiftieth Street?

KERRY. OK.

KUNSTLER. So, I figure, I'm going to be at Caroline's for this party. My party. In the spirit of the place, I'm thinking of doing a few minutes.

KERRY. Of?

KUNSTLER. Comedy.

KERRY. Of course.

KUNSTLER. Stand up.

KERRY. And this relates to here—how?

KUNSTLER. I figure—we've got an audience here. Maybe try out a few jokes. What do you think?

 A beat.

KERRY. That's entirely up to you.

KUNSTLER. Solid.

 Kerry signals the light booth and the house lights go down. She walks to the podium, switches on the podium light, and addresses the audience. So as not to be a distraction, the podium light will fade up and down significantly throughout the show during sections when Kunstler is away from the podium.

KERRY. On behalf of the program committee, I want to thank you all for coming. There are a handful of people about whom you can accurately say they need no introduction, and tonight's speaker is one of those. Those of us here who are law students, we're familiar with many of his cases. I think it's safe to say that he is one of the more controversial figures of our time. I think it's safe to say that he doesn't mind being identified as such. So please welcome William Kunstler.

> *Kunstler approaches the podium, setting his file folders, the protest pamphlet he entered with, and the yellow legal pad down. The lights adjust further, focusing on the podium. We will refer to this as the "lecture setting." Kunstler shakes hands with Kerry, who takes a seat in a chair to the side where she is visible in her own light. He does a little serious-looking fiddling behind the podium. A beat. He looks up.*

KUNSTLER. Question: What do you call a lawyer gone bad? Answer: A senator.

> *He is sufficiently pleased by the audience reaction to decide this joke is a keeper. He makes a check mark on his pad.*

Question: What do you call a lawyer with an IQ of seventy? Answer: Your Honor.

> *Kerry can't quite cover her dismay. But Kunstler figures this rates another check mark, then winks at Kerry. Kerry keeps a straight face.*

I understand I've been invited to give one of a series of seminars. Many of you are on track to be lawyers, and—aside from whatever you're gleaning from your classwork—the school thought you might derive some benefit from a few reports from the field. People who make their livings actually doing this. So I'm here to represent—the angels. Under the equal time principle, someone else should drop by to speak for the other side. But I understand Roy Cohn is dead these days.

> *When he refers to "the other side," he uses his fingers as horns on either side of his head. Throughout the show whenever he refers to Roy Cohn, he will make this gesture.*

Which reminds me—Question: What's the difference between a good lawyer and a great lawyer? Answer: A good lawyer knows the law. A great lawyer knows the judge.

Kunstler makes another check on the legal pad. Kerry continues to try to look unfazed.

And speaking of Roy Cohn—he was a classmate of mine. Yes. At Columbia. Some years later, we're out of school—back before we got out of the habit of sending each other Chanukah cards—I'm doing a lot of work on trusts and estates. Probably in the early fifties. He calls—Roy—asks me would I draft a will for a buddy of his. And I did. At the time, I was flattered—I mean, a United States senator! We all respect senators, right? So yes, I drafted a will for Joseph McCarthy.

He comes out from behind the podium and approaches the audience. As he does he is subtly clenching and unclenching his fingers, lightly snapping them. It is a barely noticeable first indication of the symptoms of his heart disease.

Anyway, you're all sitting here and you've got your plans. You're going into the law. "The law." Sounds like it's one huge, uniform—no inconsistencies, no contradictions. Something handed to us mere mortals on a chunk of polished marble by the gods. Like one of those slabs in, you know the film…

He sings the beginning of Also sprach Zarathustra.

It's easy to think that way when you're starting out.

Sound of demonstrators chanting rises again to a noticeable level. Kunstler goes back to the podium and grabs the flyer as he speaks.

Before we get too far into this, I want to address the fact—I am aware that there are some very earnest people outside, perhaps even some of your classmates—who have handed you flyers. Flyers that urge you to boycott me, this little presentation of mine. I haven't quite figured out whose perspective they represent. I don't know if you have a Young Republicans Club on this campus. On the other hand, some labeling themselves militant Jews, they aren't completely thrilled with the fact I've defended Muslims. I am aware that I have offended people. I am aware that there are some who don't much like the kind of law I have practiced. They don't like a lot of the people I have defended. They don't like my politics. They don't like me period.

But I urge you, read these flyers very carefully. Whoever they are from. Please overlook whatever misspellings and errors in grammar—But read them. Give them the respect of considering the case they put forward against me. If, at the end of our time together, you think that their case has merit, I urge you to follow your consciences and boycott me. Retroactively.

The sound of the demonstrators begins fading out.

It may surprise you to know I did have a life before "the law." World War II. I was in the service. The Pacific. Ended up a major. I get out. My brother Michael is going to law school, and I think, sounds good. I go to law school and I set up a practice with him—with Michael—and I'm living a nice, comfortable Westchester life.

Lighting keyed to Westchester.

Married to a woman named Lotte. Two lovely daughters. Nice house. Lotte and I, we're what you might call "concerned." Parlor liberals. We join the right progressive organizations. I'm not putting them down. They make it possible for people with good intentions to feel connected, be useful. Write checks, attend benefits. The Urban League. The NAACP.

> *As he continues to speak, he riffles through his folders until he finds the one marked NAACP. He opens it and takes some papers out.*

It's the NAACP connection that gets me involved in my first civil rights case. This is sometime in the mid-fifties. Paul Redd—he's the head of the local NAACP chapter. Black gentleman. Thinks he'd like to live in the town of Rye. Rye, New York. Funny thing, every time he goes to look at a likely apartment—something listed as on the market—somehow when he shows up it's no longer available. "Hello, I'm here to see—" "Sorry, already rented!" This happens time and again, you can't blame him for getting a little—suspicious? He asks a lawyer named Zuber to help him file a discrimination suit, and Zuber asks me to lend a hand. I say sure. What we do—and we didn't invent this tactic—what we do is we send in white applicants to look at a given apartment. This establishes that it is indeed available. Then we immediately send a black applicant to look at the same apartment. If he's told it's been rented, it's evidence— legally admissible evidence—of housing discrimination. So we do this for Paul Redd. All goes as planned, we win, and Paul and his wife get their apartment in Rye. Hurrah. The system works. This time. And, at night, I get to sleep in my own bed in Westchester. I mostly sleep in my own bed for the first twelve years I practice.

And then, one morning, I get a phone call that rouses me from… whatever the hell I was dreaming. It's six A.M., June 15, 1961. A call from the ACLU. Will I drop everything, grab a plane for Jackson, Mississippi? They have a mission for me.

Lighting for Jack Young section.

So I fly to Jackson, and the next morning I sail into the law office of Jack H. Young—a black lawyer—in Jackson, Mississippi, in 1961, right?—I sail into his office with glad tidings and moral support. That's my mission. Glad tidings. "I bring you regards from the American Civil Liberties Union." To which he replies, "Fuck the American Civil Liberties Union." If I want to actually be useful, he tells me, I should get my butt over to the Greyhound terminal. A group of young people will be arriving on a bus soon. These young people are going to get off the bus, go into the terminal and try to order a meal at the lunch counter. There's going to be a reception committee— what calls itself, with unintended irony, local law enforcement.

> *Not that he makes a big deal of this, but Kunstler feels his fingers tingling again about this point and tries to shake it off so that nobody will notice.*

I go to the terminal. The bus arrives. And the Freedom Riders— that's what they were called, Freedom Riders, you've probably heard the term—they get off the bus, they go to the lunch counter, they ask to be served. Hamburgers, Cokes, fries. Five people. Three white women, one white man, one black man.

> *Here again he identifies Kerry as "black." He will continue to endow Kerry with the identity of all minorities and many of the people he is defending through all his stories. She becomes a little weary of being turned into a prop like this, but chooses not to object. Kunstler does this without irony and without*

17

intending any disrespect. He simply does it.

Now, if the whites only wanted to have lunch, there wouldn't have been a problem. But the fact that they want to have a good American lunch in the company of a "Negro," that crosses a line. That breaks a local law. A Jackson police captain asks them to leave. They don't. He arrests them and hauls them off to jail.

Now, obviously the idea is to get them out of jail. But nothing in my background has prepared me. You don't go from drafting wills to—in the blink of an eye—bending bars with your bare hands. I go back to Jack Young. Right now he's the only lawyer for all the Freedom Riders who've been arrested by other not-so-welcoming committees. Pretty much all of the sympathetic Southern lawyers have been intimidated out of defending these people. They've been threatened with beatings, disbarment, economic shit. Some of them have even left the state. So he's it. Jack. He's the only legal defense for something like four hundred Freedom Riders. And now, to add to his burden, me.

Yes, I think he's glad for my help, but I am a burden. Me and my... what?—naïveté?

Give you a taste of what he's up against: I get this idea—I blush—

> *Shift to Barnett lighting. He places Barnett at the back of the house.*

—this idea that maybe if I have a conversation with the governor of Mississippi...Ross Barnett. The two of us, you know. One on one, Ross and me. He's a veteran, I'm a veteran. He's a lawyer, I'm a lawyer. So much in common. So I get an appointment with him to see if we can figure something out. Us two guys. Yes, I'm this Jew from the North and he's...what he is. But in a private place where we can just talk like people... So I'm in his office and he asks me if I have children. That's a nice human question, right? Good beginning. So I tell him, yes, I have two daughters. And he asks me, "What would you think if your daughter married a dirty, kinky-headed, field-hand nigger?" So, if you're looking to thank or blame someone for getting me started—That is probably the moment I decide to put down the pom-poms, get on the field and play.

18

The Freedom Riders are charged with breaching the peace. This is a misdemeanor. So where else—if you're what passes for law in Mississippi—do you put these people? Parchman Penitentiary. Maximum security. *(Adopting roles.)* "What you in for?" "Assault with a deadly weapon. What you in for?" "Murder and unlawful congress with livestock. You there, kid, what you in for?" "Trying to buy a Coke."

Now, this is where I have to tip my hat to Bill Higgs. Another lawyer from Mississippi. He finds this old federal statute. It's on the tip of my tongue...

> *Kunstler looks toward Kerry as he apparently grasps for the name. Kerry picks up his cue, as he knew she would.*

KERRY. The removal statute.

KUNSTLER. Yes, thank you. You're familiar with—?

KERRY. I've done some reading in the area...

KUNSTLER. Terrific. What can you tell us about it? The removal statute?

KERRY. You want me to...

KUNSTLER. Yes. Please.

> *He encourages her to rise. She does, reluctantly.*

KERRY. Well, as I recall, it was a statute dating from the Reconstruction era...

KUNSTLER. Yes, 1866. And that statute involved...?

> *Kunstler seems to lose his balance for a second. He sits beside Kerry and rubs his left hand as she speaks.*

KERRY. If you had a case that was going to be tried in a state court, but you had reason to, uh, *grounds* to believe that you wouldn't get a fair trial there, on the state level, then you could invoke the statute.

> *Kerry starts to sit but is stopped by Kunstler.*

KUNSTLER. And what would be the advantage of that?

KERRY. You'd be able to have the case *removed* from state jurisdiction to federal jurisdiction. "Removed," which is why it was called the removal statute.

KUNSTLER. And what else?

KERRY. It also required them—the authorities—required them to set bail for the defendants. They were *obliged* to set bail. And that got them out. The defendants.

KUNSTLER. That's exactly right. Very good.

> *As though she were an audience volunteer in a magic show, Kunstler leads the audience in polite applause for Kerry. She sits. He begins to speak as if he's sharing this largely with her. Kerry listens with particular attention to this passage.*

And that's how we get a lot of the Freedom Riders out of places like Parchman. No sooner do Freedom Riders get arrested by a local authority, we fly in, invoke the removal statute, and get their cases moved to federal and get them out. The local authorities? They don't know what hit them. We got a lot of people out. There are those who think keeping people out of those jails saved the movement. It was quite a time, to be… To be directly engaged in what you knew was going to change lives, change the face of the country. Because you sure don't do this kind of work for money. No, if you want to make money, don't look to me as a role model. Not that I suggest you should look to me as a role model in any case. Though you could do worse.

> *Kunstler makes the horns on either side of his head, looks directly at Kerry, and prompts her. It is clear he will not move on until she answers.*

KERRY. Roy Cohn?

> *Kunstler is delighted.*

KUNSTLER. I know it's not seemly to speak ill of the dead, but shall we?

> *He rises to address the audience.*

OK, I was talking about… Yes, right. The removal statute as a tool. This was the beginning of my understanding what Jack Young was trying to teach me. A different idea of the law. Not as this slab of marble but as something that moves and mutates and changes shape. A little like in that old monster movie—*The Blob*. Movement law. That's the term for it. Movement law. Means our loyalty, as lawyers, is not to some abstract ideal. It's to serve the political objectives of our clients.

Give you an example.

Kunstler picks up a folder full of papers.

Some years later, in 1968, I was defending these two priests—the Berrigan brothers—and some others—they were called the Catonsville Nine—defending them for destroying what was called, again with unintended irony, government property. The "property" was the draft records of a hundred and sixty-five young men.

> *He dumps the pages, representing the files of the young men he's referencing. They scatter around the stage.*

The "property" was the future of those young men and whether they might be sent to fight and maybe to die in Vietnam. "Property." Right. Now they—the Berrigans and their friends—they were guilty. They did indeed burn those records. With homemade napalm.

> *He mimes setting them on fire.*

Nice touch. And then they waited. They waited to be—they *expected* to be arrested. They *wanted* to be arrested, like some of the kids Jack and I defended in the South. Ostensibly those kids and the Berrigans—and, preview of coming attractions, others we'll get to— *ostensibly* they are being tried for breaking the law. But the tactic here is to turn the focus away from them and onto the law itself, see? The law as it was being *used* by the system. So, whereas a lawyer operating under conventional priorities might look to cut a deal, avoid a trial, maybe get a lighter sentence, the Berrigans *wanted* the trial. They saw the trial as a way to bring the issues to the—to *dramatize*, you see? To put the law itself on trial. Which is what I did to the best of my ability. They went to jail, yes. They *expected* to go. But I had served the—what I said—their political objectives. Movement law. Using our understanding of the law to serve what we think are higher goals.

> *He reaches down again—with some difficulty—to pick up the pages he dropped. Kerry moves to help him, but he waves her off again.*

Now, some years later, the Supreme Court issues a ruling that pretty much invalidates what Jack and I used in the South—the removal statute. But it's like a lot of tools. It was useful for a while, then it wore out its usefulness. And you find other tools. The law as a living thing.

As he continues to speak he goes back to the podium to replace the NAACP folder and get the Chicago Seven folder.

I'm doing this work with a few others, springing Freedom Riders, and—maybe the biggest compliment of my career—Martin Luther King asks if I would be interested in being what he calls his special trial counsel. Every now and then, when a problem comes up that he thinks I'm in a particular position to handle.

I don't pretend I was part of his inner circle. I'm not claiming that. But there were some cases he felt needed someone not smart enough to be afraid. The last thing I did for Martin…I was about to file a federal suit in support of sanitation workers. Workers Martin was supporting in a strike. I was going to go meet with him when I got the news. Martin had gone down there to where the workers were striking, to Memphis. This was April 1968. We didn't get to keep that appointment.

A beat. He checks his joke list.

What's the difference between a sperm and a lawyer? A sperm has one chance in six million to become a human being.

Kunstler gauges the audience reaction, happily makes a mark on his pad, and smiles at Kerry, who continues to exercise patience.

I spent seven months in Chicago because of a coin toss. There were two cases I was asked to be part of. One involved the Black Panthers in New York. The other, that was going to be tried in Chicago. Both pretty enticing. So, I have a colleague who's interested in both cases, too. We meet. We pull out a coin, give it a toss.

Smacks the palm of his hand on the top of another, then lifts and looks.

He gets the Panthers. By the way, he wins an acquittal for them on all counts. Me? I get *(Using a stoner voice.)* Abbie Hoffman and Jerry Rubin. And because of that I get sentenced to more than four years in jail for contempt of court.

Somewhat dismayed by the lack of recognition of the case, and its players, Kunstler, file folder in hand, approaches the audience to explain.

I'm looking at you and it hits me, yeah, for a lot of you this is history. OK: As a result of an enormous number of lies, both to the American people and to themselves, a series of administrations—Republicans and Democrats both—had gotten us involved in a civil war in Vietnam. North Vietnam, communist. South Vietnam, a kleptocracy. Gee, given a choice like that, which side are we going to go in on? Thousands of American troops—tens of thousands of American troops—drop on this little country, armed with explosives and napalm and the killing starts and escalates and it doesn't stop. This is the other big cause in the '60s. Fighting racism is one, and this, Vietnam, is the other. Except they're not really different causes. Lynching black people, slaughtering yellow people. In fact, sending a lot of black people to kill and be killed by yellow people.

> *Beginning under the previous paragraph, sounds of a helicopter and a single Jimi Hendrix-type electric guitar, coming from his memory rather than our reality.*

Lyndon Johnson bought into the bullshit logic of the war. Like it was quicksand and he decided to dive in head first. The 1968 election is coming and a Democratic convention is going to be held in Chicago where he's on track to be re-nominated. And then, wonder of wonders, other guys from the Democratic party show up to challenge Johnson for the nomination. A senator from Minnesota, Eugene McCarthy, runs against him in a primary—in New Hampshire—and makes a surprisingly strong showing. But then Robert Kennedy announces he's going to run, too. And now Johnson realizes he's probably in deep shit. He decides he's not going to run again. But his vice president, Hubert Humphrey, announces.

> *He does a crude imitation of Humphrey, as indeed all of his imitations tend to be energetic but crude.*

So you've got McCarthy, Kennedy, and Humphrey. Now, I have my problems with Kennedy—and that's putting it mildly—but he's saying a lot of the right stuff now, and he cuts a more striking figure than Mr. McCarthy, who, let's face it, comes across like the Stage Manager in a community theatre production of *Our Town*. But people are beginning to feel a little encouraged that someone pledged to shut down this crappy war will be nominated and elected.

But optimism gets put on a respirator in 1968. Martin Luther King is assassinated. Then Robert Kennedy is assassinated. And it looks pretty certain that Democrats from across the nation will gather in Chicago to nominate Hubert Humphrey, who—whatever he may believe privately—isn't doing much to put distance between himself and Johnson.

He walks up into the audience and uses them as the protesters.

And a lot of people—a lot of young people—think they should go to Chicago that summer to be heard. To protest! What's going to go on in the convention center is the business of death. The idea is to answer it with a festival of life. Music, street theatre, sex. But the festival of life turns out to be something else. In August, people around the world turn on their TVs and see a wave of Chicago cops beating the shit out of kids.

Kunstler gestures as though he is beating the audience.

That fall, Richard Nixon wins the election, and he decides to sic his new justice team on some of the more visible of the kids. Eight of them. Has them charged with conspiracy. The Chicago Eight. Because of that coin toss, I was one of the lawyers they asked to defend them. It was me and Leonard Weinglass.

And I have to tell you, I wasn't a kid myself. I was already in the swamps of middle age, and here I was with a group of guys who… they're not exactly laid-back guys. Particularly not Abbie Hoffman and Jerry Rubin. They think of the trial as theatre and that their part in it is comic relief. Not just for the hell of it. But to make points through calculated acts of outrageousness.

At the beginning of the trial, Jerry Rubin was bald. He was fresh from a short stretch in prison in California for anti-war activities and they clipped off all of his locks there. The guys hold a press conference and announce, *(In stoner voice.)* "Jerry Rubin is in need of hair, man!" And we start getting envelopes at the courtroom filled with hair. Hair of all different colors and textures and lengths. One day, I open an envelope, curious as to what variety today's post has fetched up. What I see is green, and it isn't hair.

He uses the file folder as the "pot" package. He opens and closes it quickly in mock surprise.

Fast as I can, I cover it with a newspaper. All those cops and marshals and agents around us, if we had been caught with it—a controlled substance, an *illegal* substance—we could have been sent to the slammer. I tell Abbie and Jerry that I think we should just leave it on the table and let the cleaning lady dispose of it.

> *He places the "pot" package on the chair next to Kerry. She gives a look to the audience suggesting she's not wild about being roped into the action again.*

"No," they insist, with very sober faces, "we must inform the judge. It is our duty."

So I get up and make a motion: "Your Honor, there was delivered to us, courtesy of your courtroom deputy, a supply of cannabis, a controlled substance under the federal code. I would like your instructions on what to do about it." The judge tells me that he assumes that as an attorney, an officer of the court, I can figure out a way to dispose of it. I promise him that it will be burned that night. And it was.

The judge in question shared a last name with Abbie. Hoffman. Judge Hoffman. Judge Julius Hoffman. No relation. I have particularly vivid memories of the judge, as I rose to look at him and address him every day of a very long trial. The flip description of him is that he looked and sounded a bit like an old *(Imitates Mr. Magoo.)* cartoon character. Sometimes you can't beat a flip description. *(Turning to Kerry.)* Kerry?

KERRY. Yes?

KUNSTLER. I want to ask a favor of you. I'd like you to read something with me.

KERRY. With you?

KUNSTLER. I have a kind of dialogue I've edited. Material from the Chicago trial. I could read it all myself, but I think it will work better if you read the other part. I'd really appreciate it. What do you say, Kerry? Give me a hand?

> *A beat.*

KERRY. All right.

> *He signals for her to take a position behind the podium. She does, with some reluctance. He takes off his coat and puts it*

around her shoulders as if a judicial robe. He hands her pages. As he speaks he rearranges the chairs in front of the podium—one to the right, one to the left—to suggest a courtroom. The Chicago Eight/Seven section light evokes the bareness of courtroom lighting: The walls of the stage take on a harder appearance. Kunstler will travel back and forth between the "defense table"—stage left of podium—and the "witness stand"—stage right of podium—as he plays the various characters.

KUNSTLER. Just read the lines marked "Judge Hoffman." Reach down and find that little old Jewish man hiding inside you.

KERRY. OK.

Kunstler crosses behind the chair standing for the defense table.

KUNSTLER. *(Back to audience.)* September 26, 1969. I'm making my opening statement: *(Reading.)* "We hope to prove before you that this prosecution which you are hearing is a result of two motives on the part of the government—"

He looks to Kerry.

This is where he interrupted—the judge.

KERRY. You want me to—

KUNSTLER. Just jump in. When you see a dash, just do what he did. Jump in. *(To Kerry.)* I've just said the part about the two motives on the part of the government—

KERRY. "You may speak…"

Kunstler interrupts and coaches her into doing the Mr. Magoo voice.

KUNSTLER. *(Magoo voice.)* "You may speak…"

KERRY. *(Trying her best.)* "You may speak…"

She then goes back to her own voice as she reads further.

"…To the guilt or innocence of…"

Kunstler stops her again and repeats it in Magoo voice.

KUNSTLER. *(Magoo voice.)* "…To the guilt or innocence of…"

Kerry gives him a dismayed look. Kunstler gives up and motions for her to go on. Which she does in her own voice.

KERRY. *(Reading.)* "You may speak to the guilt or innocence of your clients, not to the motive of the government."

KUNSTLER. "The defendants are charged with conspiracy. The defense will show that the *real* conspiracy in this case is a conspiracy against the rights of everybody, all of us American citizens, to protest against the war that was brutalizing us all." *(To audience.)* Judge Hoffman and the prosecution want to frame this as narrowly as possible—as a criminal trial. For us—the defendants and my co-counsel, Mr. Weinglass—it's a political trial. Later in the proceedings the judge and I have a dialogue on this.

> He cues Kerry.

KERRY. "This is not a political case as far as I'm concerned."

KUNSTLER. "Well, Your Honor, as far as some of the rest of us are concerned, it is *quite* a political case."

KERRY. "It is a criminal case. I have the indictment right up here. I can't go into politics here in this court."

KUNSTLER. "Your Honor, Jesus was accused criminally, too, and we understand really that was not truly a criminal case—"

KERRY. "I didn't live at that time. I don't know. Some people think I go back that far, but I really don't."

KUNSTLER. "Well, I was assuming Your Honor had read of the incident." *(To audience.)* Now, one of the defendants was Bobby Seale.

> Kunstler indicates a chair as Bobby.

A co-founder of the Black Panthers.

> Kunstler realizes he needs to explain this to his young audience.

The Panthers was an organization of militant African-Americans who advocated being armed to defend themselves against police brutality. That's too short a description for something that excited so much controversy, for good reasons and bad. But by being a co-founder of an organization J. Edgar Hoover hated, he became a desirable target. The fact is, he'd spent only two days in Chicago during the convention, but Nixon's boys wanted a black face in there to scare America. Bobby chose his own lawyer—Mr. Charles R. Garry. But Mr. Garry was in the hospital recovering from surgery on his gall bladder when the case began. This should have been reason to either postpone the trial or to separate his case from the others. But this railroad had a schedule, and Judge Hoffman and the prosecution weren't going to let a few legal niceties get in the way. *(To Kerry, cueing.)* That's you: "Mr. Kunstler, do you—"

KERRY. "Mr. Kunstler, do you represent Mr. Seale?"

KUNSTLER. "No, Your Honor, as far as Mr. Seale has indicated to me, because of the absence of Charles R. Garry—"

KERRY. "I will permit you to make another opening statement on behalf of Mr. Seale if you like."

KUNSTLER. "Your Honor, I cannot compromise Mr. Seale's position—If I were to make an opening statement, I would compromise his position that he has not his full counsel here. Under the circumstances, he would prefer to represent himself."

KERRY. "Mr. Seale is not to make an opening statement. I so order."

> *Kunstler directs her to slap the podium with her hand as gavel. After a beat she does.*

KUNSTLER. This is the beginning of an ongoing issue. OK— October 2, 1969: "I want the record to quite clearly indicate that I do not direct Mr. Seale in any way. He is a free independent black man who does his own direction."

KERRY. "Black or white, sir—and what an extraordinary statement, 'an independent black man.' He will be calling you a racist before you are through, Mr. Kunstler."

KUNSTLER. "Your Honor, I think to call him a free independent black man will not incite his anger."

What does incite Bobby's anger is that, not only is he denied the lawyer of his choice, he is not allowed to defend himself. Not being allowed to defend himself, he isn't allowed to leave jail and go out and interview witnesses and build a defense.

> *Kunstler now sits in the Bobby Seale seat and begins to work into Bobby's character.*

He also wants the right to cross-examine the prosecution's witnesses and argue motions and have a fair opportunity to prove his innocence. He protests his treatment loudly and often.

He shifts into what he imagines is a black accent.

Very loudly, very often. And with language like "fascist," "dog," and "pig."

> *Kerry is not unaware of the absurdity that this white man is playing a black man, badly, while she, a black woman, is playing an old white man. Kunstler cues Kerry, and she begins to read.*

KERRY. "I find that to allow the defendant Seale to act as his own attorney would produce a disruptive effect. On the contrary, the complexity of the case makes self-representation inappropriate, and the defendant would be more prejudiced were he allowed to conduct his own defense."

> *Kunstler indicates Kerry should pound the podium again. She does.*

KUNSTLER. And Bobby replies, *(Black voice.)* "My lawyer is not here. I think I have a right to defend myself in this courtroom. The Federal Code says the black man cannot be discriminated against in his legal defense in any court in America."

> *Kerry is disturbed by Kunstler's imitation but tries to soldier on.*

KERRY. "Mr. Seale, you want to stop or do you want me to direct the marshal—"

KUNSTLER. *(Black voice.)* "I want to argue the point."

KERRY. "Take that defendant into the room there and deal with him as he should be dealt with in this circumstance."

KUNSTLER. *(Shouting in black voice as he pretends to be dragged off.)* "I still want to be represented. I want to represent myself." The marshals drag him out. When we see Bobby again, he is bound to a chair with a gag in his mouth. Incredible, huh, Kerry?

> *A beat.*

KERRY. Incredible.

> *Kerry is commenting on Kunstler and his performance.*

KUNSTLER. But this is what we were facing in those days, this kind of—

KERRY. In those days.

KUNSTLER. Well, God knows, there are still battles to be won.

A beat.

Judge Hoffman tries to justify his action to the jury.

Kunstler cues Kerry.

KERRY. "Ladies and gentlemen, in a trial by jury in a federal court, the judge is not a mere moderator under the law but is the governor of the trial. The law requires that the judge maintain order and accordingly, the marshals have endeavored to maintain order in the manner you see here in the courtroom."

KUNSTLER. "Your Honor, I move for the seven defendants other than Mr. Seale for the removal of the irons and the gag, on the ground that he was attempting only to assert his right to self-defense under the Constitution…"

KERRY. "The motion of Mr. Kunstler will be denied."

Kunstler prods Kerry to bang the podium. She does.

KUNSTLER. "This is absolutely medieval."

KERRY. "The record does not indicate that I could stop Mr. Seale."

KUNSTLER. "You can, Your Honor. He asks one thing of you and that is the right to defend himself."

KERRY. "You are his lawyer—"

KUNSTLER. "I am *not* his lawyer—"

KERRY. "—and if you are any kind of a lawyer you would continue to do it."

KUNSTLER. "If I were any kind of a lawyer I would protest against what is being done in this courtroom and I am so protesting on behalf of the other seven defendants in this case."

KERRY. "Why should I have to go through a trial and be assailed in an obscene manner?"

KUNSTLER. "But, Your Honor, that is a reaction of a black man not being permitted to defend himself. If you had said to him, 'Defend yourself,' none of this would have happened."

KERRY. "I have had black lawyers in this courtroom who tried cases with dignity and with ability. His color has nothing to do with his conduct."

KUNSTLER. "We feel—as human beings—that it is impossible to continue this trial with a black man in chains." *(To audience.)* Finally, when he recognizes it's impossible to proceed like this, the judge separates Bobby's case from the proceedings. The Chicago Eight become the Chicago Seven.

> *Kunstler crosses back to his defense table. For a second, he is light-headed and loses his balance. He grips the chair. But he recovers and makes no reference to it, just going on.*

One of the witnesses we planned on calling was Ramsey Clark. Clark was attorney general for President Johnson, and he was prepared to testify that, when he was attorney general, the Justice Department had *no* plans to prosecute the leaders of the Chicago demonstration. You can imagine the impact it would have had to have the previous attorney general testifying for the defense in a case brought by his successor. Judge Hoffman—ready for a surprise?— says that Clark could make "no relevant or material contribution" to the case and refuses to allow him to take the stand.

We also planned to call the Reverend Ralph Abernathy, a leading civil rights figure. The last day of our defense, he is on his way to the courtroom but is delayed. Now the judge refuses to grant us a brief recess to give the reverend time to get there. Instead he says to the jury—

KERRY. "I must inform you that I have called on the defendants to produce whatever witness they had, and they have had none ready to proceed, and they did not indicate that they would rest. Hence, I let the record show in your presence that the defendants have rested."

> *For the first time Kerry takes the initiative, banging on the podium without his prompting. Kunstler nods his approval.*

KUNSTLER. "Your Honor, I'm going to say my piece right now, and you can hold me in contempt if you wish to. You violated every principle of fair play when you excluded Ramsey Clark from that witness stand. I know that it doesn't mean much in this court, but the former attorney general of the United States walked out of here with his lips so tight he could hardly breathe. If you had seen the expression on his face! The *New York Times* called it the ultimate outrage in American justice. As for me? I haven't been able to get this out before, and I am saying it now, and then put me in jail if you want to. I feel disgraced to be here. I have watched the objections denied and sustained by Your Honor, and I know that this is not a fair trial. I know it in my heart. If I have to lose my license to practice law and if I have to go to jail, I can't think of a better cause to go to jail for. I am going to turn back to my seat with the realization that everything I have learned throughout my life has come to naught, that there is no meaning in this court, and there is no law in this court."

> *Kunstler is emotional and impressed reading his own words. He pauses to proudly show this page to an audience member. He crosses up to podium and takes his legal pad of "jokes" and reads—*

OK, this one's a classic: A judge asks a particularly feisty lawyer, "Are you trying to show contempt for this court?" And the lawyer replies, "No, Your Honor, I'm trying to hide it."

> *Kunstler cheerfully makes a big check beside that joke and shares his joy with Kerry. During this next stretch, we should gradually shift from the Chicago lighting back to the lecture lighting. When, shortly, Kerry moves from behind the podium and takes her seat, that seat will be closer to the podium and will remain there. Lights should adjust to include her in that position.*

Judge Hoffman sentences me to four years and thirteen days in prison for twenty-four different occasions in which I couldn't hide contempt. Later, the U.S. Court of Appeals dismisses the charges. The jury finds the Seven not guilty of conspiracy, but convicts five of them of crossing state lines to incite. In 1972, the appeals court overturns *all* of the convictions, specifically referring to Judge Hoffman's refusal to allow Ramsey Clark to testify. The government decides not to take any further actions against the defendants.

> *Kunstler takes his coat off of Kerry. He addresses the audience, using his jacket as the physical manifestation of the "judge as tyrant" below.*

But by the end, I find that the trial has changed me. It has been the shock of my life. For years, I had looked to the federal court, *relied* on it, to seek redress for injustice. But here was a federal court where the judge acted as a tyrant, the prosecutors exhibited open malice, and—in collusion with the prosecution—witnesses perjured themselves.

> *He nods his thanks to Kerry and directs her to be seated again.*

At the end of the process, the fact that finally, *finally* the defendants are cleared does not hide the truth I am compelled to confront: The judicial system in this country is *part* of the machinery of established power, and it is often unjust and it will punish those whom that power hates or fears.

> *Kunstler crosses to podium, replaces Chicago Seven folder, and picks up Attica folder. As he crosses downstage the podium light fades to dim.*

In 1971, I'm asked to be a member of a citizens' committee. One of a number of observers whose presence, it is hoped, will keep a lot of people from being killed. And so I fly to upstate New York.

My first look at that building. It's a cliché, I know, but if you saw it what other words would you use but grim and gothic?

> *For the most part, during the Attica passage, Kunstler will be downstage center, using the audience as the prisoners in the yard, so the light should imply the tight, overcrowded conditions of angry men trapped in a small space. The side walls of the stage will become a dark and looming presence behind Kerry. Sound will be a computer-generated sound—an audio manifestation of the "tension of potential energy" of which Kunstler speaks, like a tightening spring. The sound of it will rise and fall during this passage.*

Approaching Attica as a civilian, you can't help but think what it must be like to enter it for the first time as an inmate. Maybe a young black or Latino man. You've gotten into trouble in the city. You've been arrested, tried, sentenced. And here you are, far from anything you've ever known, out in the middle of nowhere. Inside—you're jammed. The place was built to hold sixteen hundred, you find yourself packed in with twenty-two hundred. Like I say, you're probably black or Latino. The guards?

Kunstler points up and indicates the guards surrounding them from above as the lights tighten around him.

No black faces. As I remember, one Latino guard out of, what?— more than four hundred. And these four hundred, they've been raised mostly in a white, rural, upstate world, and you— *(Indicating the audience.)* —a kid from the streets—come in and to them you look like something alien and threatening. Add to this that, as a result of the upheaval of the '60s, there are lots of people serving time with you whose politics are part of why they're there— Panthers, Weathermen, Young Lords, Muslims. Many of them have their own awareness, their own pride. Some are better read, better educated than the guards. Now, I'm not entirely without sympathy for some of the guards. It's hard to exert authority over prisoners who feel they are superior to you. So the whole place—

In physics—maybe you remember this from high school—there's something called P.E.—potential energy. Say you've got a big spring, and it's all coiled and compressed, quivering. There's a restraining force holding it in, but if that restraining force is removed, blam. Scientists know how to measure this P.E. when you're talking about springs or a volcano or a roller-coaster just about to drop down an incline. It happens in people, too, of course. The force building up inside, the pressure created by rage and frustration, and it builds and builds. I don't know that scientists have any way of measuring this in people, but it's the same principle. If that restraining force is dislodged…

Now we get to one particular restraining force. It's a gate. A group of twenty or so inmates—riled up by a run-in between a guard and a prisoner that flashed and escalated—they begin pulling and banging on this gate. This gate I'm talking about—

As he describes the gate he creates it, with his arms becoming the span of the "rod in question" and his fingers the short rod with the extension added.

—it's supposed to be held in place by a steel rod that's supposed to go six inches into both the floor and the ceiling. But when they were building it—building Attica—the rod in question was made too short. So rather than do it over—do it over *right*—someone,

someone in charge of construction thought they'd save a couple of bucks. So they welded on a piece of metal to the end of the rod as an extension. But that weld isn't strong enough. So comes this day in September, these guys are yanking and banging on the gate…

Kunstler mimes pushing at the door until it breaks.

…the rod snaps at the weak point, and suddenly it flies open, releasing all that energy that is potential no longer. Three guards are nearby, and the prisoners grab broomsticks and baseball bats and visit their rage on them. The name of one of the guards is William Quinn.

From here, the prisoners get hold of a set of keys and they end up controlling much of the prison, including one of the yards—D yard. And they take hostages—

Kunstler illustrates by reaching around Kerry from behind and uses his hand as a shiv.

—guards and some civilians who have the bad luck to be there. So they have hostages, they feel they have something to negotiate with. Something to make the authorities talk to them. And they want observers as part of this. Which is how I get that phone call and why I take that flight. I arrive at the prison itself. It's around midnight when I and some of the other observers are taken inside. We are escorted into D yard, which is a big open area where they've put up a table.

He indicates the "table" down center at the edge of the audience. Kunstler grabs the free chair, places it at the "table," and sits facing the inmates.

And that's where we sit, at the table, facing them. Facing something like twelve hundred guys. Each of us observers—and it's an interesting group, including Congressman Herman Badillo; Clarence Jones, the publisher of the *Amsterdam News*; and Tom Wicker from the *New York Times*—anyway, each of us is asked to make a statement.

When it comes my turn, I have to tell you—I look at this huge crowd of men who have seized power from a system that has systematically degraded them, and I am hit with the full weight of the fact that they have asked us to be there. Asked *me* to be there.

One of them, a man named Flip Crowley, seems to know about my run-in with Judge Hoffman and my contempt citations. He yells out, "Brother Kunstler, what did they do with you in court?" And I go, "The same thing they did with you, brother!" And we hug.

He reaches out and hugs the air across the "table," miming the famous picture of that moment.

And there's a cheer. And suddenly, by acclamation, they ask me to be their lawyer. In the flash of one moment I have twelve hundred clients.

But the question is—what can I do for them?

Some of the things proposed are just not going to—I mean, nobody's going to supply jets to fly them all to asylum in North Vietnam.

Kunstler takes a couple of pieces of paper out of the Attica folder. They are aged, and crumpled, and stapled together—it is a copy of one of the drafts of the handwritten demands from Attica.

But most of what comes up as we go over the issues are straightforward, common-sense proposals for prison reform. Stuff like having more guards and doctors who can speak Spanish. How can people expect to deal with each other if they don't understand each other? And hiring some black guards. Putting together serious educational and rehabilitation programs so they have a chance to come out with skills to find work. A process for the airing of grievances. More recreational facilities. An effective narcotics treatment program. Minimum wage for work done. True religious freedom. Not a very radical list.

I'm part of an executive committee. We hammer the various proposals into a document of twenty-eight points. And we're dealing with the state correction commissioner and he actually says he will accept them. But the question is whether *my clients* will accept them. Because there's something missing on that list that they want: amnesty for the uprising.

One of the other people my clients want involved is a fellow veteran of Chicago—Bobby Seale. The Panther connection. If he endorses the twenty-eight points, I think they will listen to him. I think there's a chance they will release the guards and we can bring this to a peaceable end. I call him and he flies in.

I don't mind telling you I'm getting scared. The tension is building among the guys in the yard. The threat of violence hums around me and the other observers when we go in there. The agitation is also building in the crowds of guards and cops and families of prisoners and hostages outside. It's like this is another gate that is being subjected to all this pressure.

> *He now shepherds an unseen Bobby into the yard. He places Bobby in the downstage chair and stands just behind, watching the interaction he describes.*

Bobby and I go into the yard. He speaks to them very quietly. He tells them he wants to take the list—the twenty-eight points—back to the central committee of the Panthers for discussion.

> *Kunstler is clearly frustrated by this.*

Sometimes you lead not because you grab the power to lead. Sometimes you lead because people *give* you the power, they *make* you a leader. I mean, I didn't *ask* to become their lawyer. Well, I think the men in that yard wanted to make Bobby a leader, and he didn't want to accept the responsibility of that power. One of the objections he and the Panthers had with Martin Luther King is that Martin was pretty much a one-man show. He decided what was going to be done and people followed. But the Panthers put a lot of store in sharing decision-making. And that's what Bobby wanted to do with the twenty-eight points. And, you know, it's great when you have the luxury of time to do that. But he didn't have that time. The men wanted to hear his take on the points, and he wouldn't step out on his own and say what I think he could have said. Instead, he's there for maybe five minutes. Very quiet, low key. He mentions about consulting with his committee, and he leaves.

> *Kunstler crosses, indicates Bobby leaving. A beat.*

I escort him back outside. While I'm doing that, Clarence Jones, the editor of the *Amsterdam News*—he's still in the yard. He begins reading the twenty-eight points. They—some of the prisoners—they start calling out, "What about the amnesty? Is that in there?" But he doesn't answer directly. He keeps reading. And then, when he gets to the end of it, the men hear that amnesty is *not* in the document, the men begin to hoot and jeer. One of them runs to the table, grabs the paper from him and rips it up. I've returned to the yard. Tom Wicker tells me he thinks they're angry enough that they might kill us all. Someone yells, "What does Kunstler think about it?"

I step forward to the microphone.

> *Kunstler approaches the center chair and puts a foot on it as if to stand, but stops himself.*

There's a part of me that just wants to save my own hide. And I think that the safest thing is for me to say what they want me to say. To tell them they're right to tear up the list. That might buy us the time to get our asses out of the yard intact. But I can't do it. If I'm their lawyer, then they have a right to hear my best advice.

> *Kunstler finally stands on the chair and addresses the audience as prisoners.*

I tell them, "You have the absolute right to turn this down. But we have worked and fought very hard and the twenty-eight points are real advances. No, it's not everything you or we want, but it's the best I can do. You asked me to be your lawyer. As your lawyer, I do recommend you accept this and let the hostages go."

And I have to tell them why amnesty is out of the question. William Quinn, one of the guards who was beaten, has died of his injuries. There is a giant gasp. Everyone knows that this changes the game. There is no way that the state can consider amnesty now.

Now, I say, "It's up to you to decide what you want to do."

> *Kunstler gets down from the chair and stands in silence for a beat.*

I keep going back to that moment, wondering if there was something more I could have done or said.

> *A beat.*

And Wicker and Jones and the rest of us leave D yard.

But there is one possibility left. There was one person who, if he showed up and said—what?—that he took the prisoners' concerns seriously. Showed them some degree of respect.

During the following section, lighting and sound that reflect the contrasting world of the dinner party—clinking of champagne glasses, etc.

I get invited to a lot of dinner parties, and I do enjoy going to them. The food is usually good, and you often meet people you otherwise wouldn't meet. A couple of years after Attica, I find myself seated at a table, and the woman next to me says, "Why did you call my father a murderer?" She turns out to be Mary Rockefeller, the daughter of Nelson Rockefeller, the then-governor of the state of New York.

I tell her if he had come to Attica, he could have saved lives. His refusal condemned a lot of men to death. She says, "But he might have been killed if he had gone in the yard." Nobody was asking him to go into the yard, I tell her.

Kunstler points again to where he had placed the guards in the beginning.

But if he had stood above on the catwalk and used the bullhorn and said he supported the twenty-eight points—points that his representatives had already endorsed—and if he had used his prestige to promise that they would be treated fairly, that there wouldn't be mass, indiscriminate prosecutions for the death of Officer Quinn, I think that could have made all the difference.

I don't believe I persuaded Miss Rockefeller.

The dinner party atmosphere fades back into the Attica sound, suggesting tension.

But it's what I believed and still believe. I think Rockefeller was the one person with the position to pull this off, and he refused to do it. Another person who refused to lead.

During the following, Kunstler will move to a position upstage right, as though he is outside the prison walls. The stage becomes dark and foreboding. During the "pop-pop-pop" passage, flashes of lights from above suggesting the gunshots, and we hear the thin echo of gunshots—barely recognizable, but there.

Rockefeller rejects our appeal on Sunday. On Monday morning, I arrive at the prison. The officers won't let me in. State troopers have been bussed in. They are now in position on top of the buildings. Prisoners hold knives to the necks of some of the hostages. And then it begins.

I'm standing outside the prison and I hear—pop, pop-pop-pop. Each of those pops is a bullet. Some of them what they call dumdum bullets, which tear gaping holes in human flesh. Designed not to wound but to obliterate. On and on the popping goes. For ten minutes. Then it's over. And more than eighty-five are wounded, and ten hostages and thirty-three inmates lie dead.

> *The gunshots and the tension sound effect fade out as we return to the lighting associated with the prison. Kunstler walks through the prison yard, stepping over bodies as he speaks, referencing Kerry as he does so.*

A spokesman comes out and announces that the firing began when the prisoners started slitting the hostages' throats. That's what he says. It's a lie. It turns out that not a single hostage died of a knife wound. They all died from bullets. Bullets fired from guns in the hands of state police who simply started shooting indiscriminately into clouds of tear gas. Many of the wounds entered the men through their backs. According to the medical examiner, some of these were lying down in surrender on the ground. I repeat: The troopers not only killed inmates, they slaughtered correction officers. The murderers that day wore uniforms and they had state-issued weapons and ammunition.

Afterwards, surviving prisoners were tortured. This is not me claiming this. This is the finding of official investigations. Later, one inmate is awarded four million dollars by a jury appalled by his treatment at the hands of officers in the wake of the assault on Attica.

> *The podium light fades back up, we shift back into the lecture lighting again. Drained of energy, he returns to the podium, places the Attica folder down, and pours himself a glass of water. He raises his glass in a toast to the area above where he had placed Rockefeller with a bullhorn.*

Governor Nelson Rockefeller of New York.

> *He now raises his glass in the direction of Gov. Ross Barnett.*

Governor Ross Barnett of Mississippi. No, I haven't had good experiences with governors. Chicago, Attica—so-called law enforcement going nuts in both places. These people whose job it is to maintain order. Well...

Kunstler seems depleted. He takes another large swig of water then replaces the glass to the shelf inside the podium. After a beat, he vamps for time. He looks at his "jokes."

OK, this isn't a lawyer joke, just a story. Because of the circles I move in, I know a fair number of writers. At a certain point, when they get successful enough, some of them rent studio apartments to use as offices, places to work away from home. But, as it happens, a lot of them don't just write there. A lot of them use these offices for other purposes. More than one marital crisis has begun with the renting of an office. So: Word gets around that this one married writer friend of mine, call him Larry, has decided *he's* going to get an office. To which a woman I know says—"Larry? You've got to be kidding. He's too ugly to have an office."

Kerry, who has remained stone-faced to his jokes up to this point, begins to laugh despite herself. He is delighted.

Now I have to tell you that in a lot of ways, I'm kind of a square. I did go to Woodstock. Yes, I was there, with Abbie and Jerry. I suppose that scores some points on the meter of cool, but, as impressed and moved as I was by the spirit there—the music? Hendrix? The Who? Yes, I know they are gods to a lot of people. As for me, give me "Some Enchanted Evening." I thank Abbie and Jer for the invitation and the experience, but when it starts to rain and it turns into Mudstock, I take that as my cue to leave. On the other hand, if they ever decide to throw a festival of Puccini, Cole Porter and Rodgers and Hart...

He sings a few bars of Rodgers and Hart's "Falling in Love with Love" or some such.* Now he seriously loses his balance and makes it to the chair. As he talks he rubs and slaps his legs. At this point—let's call it the Apologia—we shift into a limbo-like reflection of his mindset, with lighting emphasizing the subjectivity of the passage.

Sex, drugs and rock and roll—the rallying cry of the '60s. Sex, drugs and... Well, we've established rock and roll isn't my scene. Drugs?

---

* See Note on Songs/Recordings at the back of this volume.

There was a period when, during times of stress, I enjoyed the consolation of pot. And I'm not going to tell you I didn't do my share of experimenting. Which brings us to the third of that triumvirate of pleasures.

> *Kerry has noticed his behavior with some concern. Off this, he remarks—*

Circulation.

I move into the city. Into Greenwich Village. I move there alone. After all the years of so much travel and separation… To look at it from Lotte's perspective, when we got married, she had every reason and right to expect a stable life with a husband who was mostly at home. But when I discovered what I was supposed to do with my life—sure, it's exciting and fulfilling for me, but she's the one left to raise the children and to cope with the house while I'm flying from one contest to another. There are weeks when she saw more of me on TV. She would have been justified to sue the movement for alienation of affection.

> *At this point, he begins to sing a section of* La Bohème—*or some other operatic passage appropriate to a moment dealing with mortality and love*—*which puzzles Kerry further. He stops singing. A beat. Concerned, Kerry goes to the podium and pours water into his glass. She crosses to him.*

And, if I'm going to be honest… When I was away, traveling, much of the time, I was dealing with people younger than I whose attitudes had been formed in a world far less inhibited than the one in which I came of age. So, here I am, as I said, swamping through middle age. And I'm away from home, and facing the prospect of an empty hotel room in a strange town, and it's very hard to say no to—offers. And… I don't.

> *He looks up to see Kerry holding the glass to him. He takes a long drink of water and returns the glass to her.*

Grazie.

> *She nods. Kerry returns the glass to the podium and takes her seat across from him. He rallies and rises, somewhat*

---

* See Note on Songs/Recordings at the back of this volume.

haltingly, to his feet again. The lights begin to slowly cross-fade out of Apologia and back into Lecture by the time he finishes quoting Shakespeare, leaving only a slight hint of "Westchester" evident.

I'm not saying I'm not responsible for my behavior. What does Hamlet say?

"I am myself indifferent honest; but yet I could accuse me of such things that it were better my mother had not borne me: I am very proud, revengeful, ambitious, with more offences at my beck than I have thoughts to put them in…"

Well, maybe that's overstating it. That Shakespeare—he can get a little hyperbolic.

"There is a tide in human events." Another good one. *Julius Caesar,* I think. *(Correcting himself.)* No:

> "There is a tide in the affairs of men,
> Which, taken at the flood, leads on to fortune;
> Omitted, all the voyage of their life
> Is bound in shallows and in miseries.
> On such a full sea are we now afloat…"

A tide there was, especially in those days, but I won't make excuses. I wasn't merely swept along by it. I did indeed take it at the flood, and, whatever else, I can't complain of a life of shallows and miseries. The marriage was over due to my actions. The last traces of, "Hi, honey, I'm home," Mr. Westchester—gone. The last traces of what I was before that phone call took me to Mississippi and summoned me out to that full sea.

So now I'm living in Greenwich Village. A community famously welcome to the unrepentant oddball, I feel right at home.

> *He walks across the stage pointing out various areas of his neighborhood.*

I get to know some of my fellow oddballs. For a while, John and Yoko—yes—live not far away. I sometimes share a pizza with them as we talk over his legal troubles. I don't tell him about my preferring "Some Enchanted Evening." I try to be a good neighbor. My dry cleaner has a legal problem, glad to help. A guy in the diner has a question about a document, why not. I once came upon a couple of panhandlers arguing over territory. I negotiated a compromise and waived the fees. I would have just put the fees in their cups, anyway. Of course, it wasn't always idyllic there. Sometimes the protesters outside my home can be a little distracting.

The sound of demonstrators on his street.

Sometimes I step outside to talk with them. Some of them just keep yelling, and they have the right to do it. Sometimes, though, when you get up close, when you go one-on-one, you can get into good conversations. I'm not saying they end up to my way of thinking, or vice versa, but we talk and sometimes the talk ends with a hug.

> *Kunstler opens his arms and makes like he's going to hug Kerry. She stiffens. He retreats with a smile and continues. The demonstrators' chanting fades out.*

But then, I will confess, I'm a hugger. I do wrap my arms around people a lot. Sometimes my friends are surprised by those I hug. This one time, I run into a federal prosecutor, a man I've confronted in court. And yes, I hug him. An activist friend, he sees this, asks, "How can you do it? How can you show affection for this guy?" Well, it's not affection, really. But a bond develops even in contest with others. You may not hold the same views, but you do share a belief: This stuff, these issues are important, important enough to be passionate about. When I first began doing work for the movement, I wouldn't speak to those people. But time passed and I couldn't keep it up. We're all human beings, after all. Except for—

He looks at Kerry, indicates the horns until she says…

KERRY. Roy Cohn.

KUNSTLER. Some people would say you shouldn't *get* too passionate, especially in a courtroom. It clouds your judgment. And maybe you can go too far. And maybe I did when, this one time, I'm getting up a pretty good head of steam, and the judge—he actually pushes me. A judge actually laying hands on a defense attorney. Judge Fred Nichol.

Ever since I tangled with old man Hoffman in Chicago, judges have tended to look at me with a certain suspicion. "What stunt is this guy gonna try to pull on me?" I've been accused of being a showman, to which I plead guilty...with an explanation. If I have an ability to attract attention, it means I can draw attention to my clients' causes. Sometimes I purposefully leverage my—notoriety?—to give these people the public consideration they deserve.

KERRY. *(Muttering under her breath.)* Right.

Kunstler hears that Kerry has muttered something.

KUNSTLER. Hm?

Kerry is embarrassed at having interrupted him.

KERRY. I'm sorry... I didn't mean to... I'm so sorry...

Kunstler is delighted she has engaged and urges her to speak.

KUNSTLER. No please. You have an opinion. I want to hear it!

Kerry is visibly uncomfortable but clarifies.

KERRY. I only meant—the idea of using your...outside of the courtroom...?

KUNSTLER. If you're on trial, your fate is being argued, *decided* in a public forum. Doesn't anybody in that position have the right to expect... If it were you, Kerry, wouldn't you want the person who is sworn to speak for you to *speak* for you with all the resources at his command? When and wherever and however it could advance your case? Of course, it depends on the case and, as we've seen, it depends on the judge. Some judges tend to not want to be dragged into that dynamic. And I suspect that was what was on Judge Nichol's mind.

> *Moving into the Wounded Knee passage, lighting that suggests the arid, dusty village with burned-out cars through which Kunstler can maneuver. The sound may feature a subtle, slow, intermittent, single Native American drumbeat and the use of a rattle reminiscent of a rattlesnake.*

OK, what happened:

> *Kunstler is at the podium getting out the Wounded Knee folder.*

This was during what was called the Leadership Trial, part of the events surrounding Wounded Knee. I'll fill in the specifics in a minute. But sometime during the proceedings, Judge Nichol—

> *As Nichol now—Kunstler cups his ear as though he is "hearing something," approaches the audience, and points at several people.*

—thinks he hears someone laugh. He thinks it's one of the Native Americans in the courtroom, in the section for the spectators. The judge—he tells the marshals to throw them out. So these eight marshals go to throw them out, and pretty soon these eight marshals are stacked up on the floor, in states of, shall we say, flickering consciousness. That's what happens when you try to take on two very tough rows of the American Indian Movement.

My reaction?

He charges the podium.

I rush the bench and start shouting: "You brought this on." As some other officers come in to remove the Indians, I yell, "Take me also!" And the judge—the sight of me rushing the bench could have triggered this, possibly—he shoves me away. A really hard push to the chest. And soon I find myself in the Ramsey County Jail. For contempt. And Margie comes flying out from New York to my rescue.

Oh: Margie. I should mention I got married again. Margie is a lawyer, too. And she flies out and springs me. And she suggests that maybe getting thrown into jail by the judge so early doesn't…bode well?

Kunstler opens the Wounded Knee folder as he speaks.

OK, the specifics I promised you. Some of you may say, "Wounded Knee? That was in, what—1890?" That was the first Wounded Knee. What would Hollywood call it? Wounded Knee I. More than two hundred unarmed Native Americans, including women and children, machine-gunned to death by the Seventh Cavalry. Who, by the way, were subsequently awarded the Congressional Medal of Honor for heroism.

Kunstler now creates the Wounded Knee court and places Dick Wilson in the chair, stage right.

Wounded Knee II is in 1973. The catalyst is named Dick Wilson. Doesn't sound like an Indian name, but he is a Native American. He is also corrupt and violent. He cons the Bureau of Indian Affairs— which is a federal agency—into recognizing him as tribal leader on the reservation. And he has goons who work over anybody they please, and generally terrorize anybody who thinks to challenge Wilson. People die mysteriously. Nobody is charged. Finally, the people living on the reservation have had enough and they appeal to AIM—the American Indian Movement—for help. So, AIM takes possession of Wounded Knee.

Hundreds of Sioux flock there—

As he describes the following, the sound of drumbeats resumes. Kunstler begins to do what he believes is a Native American dance, pointing out the cars, blockades, and trenches across the front of the stage. Kerry again has to stifle a reaction.

—to this place where their ancestors had been slaughtered—to draw attention to the need to reform or replace the government's Bureau of Indian Affairs. They position cars—burnt-out cars—as blockades. They dig trenches. They arm themselves. And they call me. And I come out to try to help them negotiate a settlement with the government.

Government forces ring the place. Something like two hundred and fifty agents, cops, Wilson's goons. Everybody armed to the teeth. It's not only Wounded Knee II, it feels like it could turn into Attica II.

Finally, after seventy-one days, I help broker an agreement between the protesters and the government, and the siege is lifted.

But, once it is over, the government reneges on the agreement. And then it arrests two of the leaders, Russell Means and Dennis Banks. The plan—to have them be the first of a number to be tried, to decimate the American Indian Movement. I'm on the team defending Russell. We begin the trial in January 1974 in St. Paul, Minnesota.

Like in Chicago, the charges they put together—they, the government—avoid anything that smacks of the political. They want to paint Russell and Dennis not as fighters for a cause, but as criminals. So they are charged with burglary, assault, obstructing law enforcement, conspiracy, theft, distributing guns... What's more, the prosecution introduces someone to testify that he was a witness to virtually every crime of which they're accused.

He indicates Louis in the stage-right chair.

The name of this witness: Louis Moves Camp. Yes, he *is* an American Indian, and he does indeed testify with great specificity and detail. And in the middle of this—

—his own mother gets up in the courtroom and starts shouting, "He's lying!" His own mother! That everything he is saying is complete and utter crap. Someone didn't get a Mother's Day card that year. But we're able to come up with the proof that Mom is the one telling the truth. We're able to establish that on the days he claims he was watching Russell and Dennis break half the laws in the book he was in fact in California. Not only that, this character, while waiting to testify—I mean literally a week or two before he's going to come in and try to sell all this bullshit—this Louis Moves Camp was accused of raping a high school girl—and pressure was put on the girl to withdraw her complaint. *And the prosecution knew it.* They knew what kind of a witness he was, how little credibility he had, and still they put this guy on the stand.

Now, I told you the judge didn't start out with much sympathy for me. But as the trial continues… Who knows where the turning point for him is? But I'll venture a guess. The judge, toward the beginning of the trial, he had issued an exclusion order. Kerry: exclusion order, in English.

KERRY. *(Knows the drill now.)* People who might be called as witnesses weren't allowed to listen to the testimony of other witnesses. A way of preventing folks from changing, altering their testimony to match what someone else has said. He's trying to protect the integrity of the testimony, right?

> *Through the following Kunstler uses a chair as witness box, notices "the door" upstage and mimes his approach to it.*

KUNSTLER. So, this one time, I'm in the middle of examining a witness, and I see—I notice—there's this door in the wall behind the judge's bench, and this door is open, just a crack. So I keep asking my questions, and the witness keeps responding, but as this is going on, I slide over to the door as soundlessly as possible, and… I yank on the knob, throw open the door, and out tumble two guys, blam, into the courtroom onto the floor. The judge naturally wants to know—who *are* these two clowns eavesdropping, defying his order? Two FBI agents. True. Two agents who are part of the FBI's attempt to help the prosecution.

The judge—big surprise—furious. And this stuff keeps happening. They mishandle files, they withhold a range of relevant evidence. They are caught actually trying to bug the defense conferences.

Drum fades out. He crosses to podium.

And finally, Judge Nichol snaps. After eight and a half months, after the government has spent millions trying to nail Russell and Dennis, the judge—Kerry, do the honors?

Kunstler hands a page to Kerry.

Here are his actual words:

He points to where she should begin reading. She starts.

KERRY. "Although it hurts me deeply, I am forced to the conclusion that the prosecution in this trial had something other than—"

KUNSTLER and KERRY. "—attaining justice foremost in its mind…"

> *She is not pleased that he is horning in, but he nods she should continue.*

KERRY. "The waters of justice have been polluted—"

KUNSTLER. *(Interrupting.)* Polluted!—

KERRY. "—have been polluted, and dismissal, I believe,—"

KUNSTLER and KERRY. "—is the appropriate cure for the pollution in this case."

KUNSTLER. He dismisses the charges.

> *Kunstler pounds the podium just as he had prompted Kerry to do.*

Russell and Dennis are free.

> *He pounds the podium again. He nods at Kerry. She looks at him wryly and sits again.*

He dismisses the charges because he is disillusioned with the behavior of the government, the government he also serves.

Here's the paradox: His disillusion, in that moment, gives me…

This is a judge who started the trial palpably unsympathetic to the defense. By the end, despite his predisposition, he declares his independence. He refuses to be part of the conspiracy.

> *Kunstler puts the pages back into the folder and carries it*

forward toward the audience.

That word, "conspiracy." People shy away from it. "Bill," they say, "so melodramatic, so over-the-top." But as it happens, about the same time we're arguing Wounded Knee, thousands of miles east Watergate has been playing out. The same administration that was trying to put Russell and Dennis away have been breaking into Democratic Party headquarters, engaging in massive cover-ups. Given all this—all well documented—it's hard to claim that the word "conspiracy" is—what—excessive?

But in that moment, I really think this might be the first step in a turnaround in America. If a federal judge—a *federal* judge—could stand up and cry foul, accuse the government of bad faith, I think maybe it is a sign a wider cleansing process could begin.

After all, this is what I've been working for. My whole career I have been working in the belief that, by using the tools of the law, I can have a hand in changing the system.

> *Kunstler, file folder in hand, arms outstretched, presents himself as the scales of justice trying to find balance.*

A change that would mean that the machine of justice wouldn't automatically be tilted to the advantage of big government, big money, the entrenched and established bullies. And, as I say, for that one moment, I allow myself to...hope.

And...it was a blip. A beautiful blip. But this was not the beginning of a new wave of enlightenment. After Wounded Knee... After Watergate—the system goes right back to what it did before, grinding down those who challenge its legitimacy.

> *He drops his arms.*

One of my friends—he says that I talk like a betrayed lover. Maybe it's not in the realm of the possible to make the whole system fairer. But in individual cases, at least, it's possible to throw a little extra weight onto one side of the scales. And so that's what I've come to. No, I won't see the system changed. But I can step up for those individuals to whom I think I can be useful.

> *Kunstler weakly makes the power fist sign in the air above his head and stands in the pose for a beat. It is now obvious*

that he is extremely tired but trying to maintain. He goes to the podium, looks for a brief moment through his folders, then, somewhat distracted, says:

I had a few more jokes I was going to try out, but I think I've covered what I was hoping to cover.

It has been a pleasure to be here today. I wish you great and good luck, and I hope you will use the skills you are acquiring in the service of the good. If you'll pardon my moralizing, there is a difference between being smart and wise. A lot of people can claim to be intelligent. But wisdom—wisdom is knowing what to do with—to what *purposes* to put whatever share of intelligence you are blessed with. In my experience, the number of the wise is smaller than the number of the smart. I hope you increase the numbers of the wise.

Thank you.

Kerry is surprised by this sudden end to the lecture—she hops up from her seat, starts—or joins—the audience applause. She goes to the podium as he steps away and takes a seat.

KERRY. I'm sure I speak for everybody when I thank Mr. Kunstler for his generosity and candor today. For those who might be interested in joining the program committee to discuss possible programs for spring 1996, we're having a meeting tomorrow at 1:30 in room 701. Refreshments will be provided. Thank you.

Lights slowly fade out of the lecture mode and imply a feeling of separateness from the body of the show. As the auditorium evidently empties, Kunstler remains seated. Kerry gets glass of water and pitcher from podium, she crosses off with it. Kunstler rises and calls after her.

KUNSTLER. Hey, do you want to come to Caroline's?

KERRY. Excuse me?

KUNSTLER. My birthday party. The comedy club. I was going to do a solo act, but we make a pretty good team, don't you think? I mean, if we can get your Judge Hoffman up to speed…

Kerry reenters.

Was it Gotti?

KERRY. I'm sorry, what?

KUNSTLER. Why you voted against inviting me. There was a reason, yes? A reason you voted the way you—So I was guessing Gotti.

KERRY. Don't you think…

She hesitates.

KUNSTLER. What?

KERRY. You came, you've given the talk. My reasons—whatever they were—

KUNSTLER. Reasons? "Reasons" plural?

KERRY. Would you like me to call you a cab?

A beat.

KUNSTLER. Just curious.

A beat. Kunstler goes to the podium to collect his papers and folders.

KERRY. Gotti… Actually, Gotti I could kind of see. The Italian stereotyping, the discrimination angle—

KUNSTLER. Not to mention his attorney of choice was stripped from him. Kind of important, don't you think?

KERRY. Though I notice you didn't bring him up in your talk, so I guess you don't think of him as one of your greatest hits.

KUNSTLER. I'm sorry?

KERRY. Like when a band puts out a record of their greatest hits— Although, you have to be very clear what you mean by "hits" when you're talking about John Gotti.

KUNSTLER. So it wasn't Gotti.

KERRY. Not the case itself, defending him. There was also a photo of you hugging him…

KUNSTLER. Well, like I say, I'm a hugger.

KERRY. Yes.

KUNSTLER. You object to my hugging John Gotti.

KERRY. A gangster.

KUNSTLER. Probably.

KERRY. Defending him is one thing, hugging him—

KUNSTLER. I see. Everyone has a right to a defense, but not everybody has a right to a hug. You might want to propose an amendment to the code of ethics.

KERRY. You have to admit it does send a—

KUNSTLER. I definitely hugged Yusef Salaam. Was *that* the straw that broke your camel?

KERRY. To go from defending the Chicago Seven, the Berrigans, Wounded Knee—

KUNSTLER. Which you see as noble causes, *worthy* causes—

KERRY. —and then a confessed rapist. A guy who confessed to being part of a pack of other guys—

KUNSTLER. —black and Latino—

KERRY. —black and Latino—

KUNSTLER. —it's important—

KERRY. But they rape and come close to killing a woman jogging in Central Park. And Yusef Salaam is one of them and he confesses—

KUNSTLER. —a fifteen-year-old boy who was questioned—if you want to call it that—by the cops without proper warning and without the presence of his family or a guardian.

KERRY. You have daughters, don't you?

> *A beat.*

KUNSTLER. I don't see what that has to do with—

KERRY. Were they proud of you defending him? Did they say, "Way to go, Dad?"

KUNSTLER. My daughters have their own opinions.

KERRY. And what was their opinion of their father about this case? A young woman is brutally attacked, and you offer your services to one of her attackers.

KUNSTLER. Alleged. But no, you're right, they weren't happy about that case.

KERRY. And they told you so.

KUNSTLER. They speak their minds. And they sometimes don't approve of the clients or the causes I take on.

KERRY. You went on television to defend a cat.

KUNSTLER. Tyrone the Cat. In a mock trial.

KERRY. A *cat*.

KUNSTLER. For crimes against humanity. It was a kind of joke.

KERRY. A stunt.

KUNSTLER. They thought—my daughters—they thought I'd lost my mind. On the other hand, they have cats for pets so they didn't want Tyrone to lose.

KERRY. And you think this was a good use of your energies?

KUNSTLER. I got to make a few larger points about nature vs. nurture, and I had some fun. Or do you disapprove of fun?

OK, "my greatest hits" as you call them—look at the times they came out of: civil rights, Vietnam, the Indian movement, the Berrigans, free speech. This campus, in 1968, students seized the buildings to protest the university's involvement in the war. Where I once saw a genuine engagement with injustice, today the passion I see is for getting to a comfy and lucrative berth on Wall Street. If you think my cases have declined in nobility, well, I can only choose from what is offered me. And so I do. They may not have the size and weight and consequence you're nostalgic for—

KERRY. I think it's a hell of a long distance from Martin Luther King to Yusef Salaam.

KUNSTLER. Not so long. They were both the object of attacks by the government. Here's what you don't—Pardon me, but I do believe it's true: There's a myth. One of the central myths of organized society: That everything that's done through the established system is legal. And that word—legal—it has a powerful psychological impact. It makes people believe that there is an order to life and an order to the system and that a person who goes through this order and is convicted has gotten all that is due to him, and therefore society can turn its conscience off and look to other things.

KERRY. You don't believe in due process?

KUNSTLER. I don't believe in putting process above people. The process is supposed to *serve* justice. The thing about these past trials— they have this aura of legitimacy, this aura of legality. I suspect that more good men have gone to their deaths through legal systems than through all the illegalities in the history of man. Six million disposed of during the Third Reich? Legal. Sacco and Vanzetti? Quite legal. The Haymarket defendants? Legal. Socrates? Jesus? The hundreds of rape trials throughout the South when black men were condemned to death? Legal. Those in power learn that it is far better to work their will through some semblance of legality. And they get away with these injustices again and again and call it—

BOTH. —due process.

KUNSTLER. So my job—what I conceive of it as—when I see the force of the government cloaking itelf in the garb of legality and going after someone who is at a particular disadvantage—whether it's because of race or some existing prejudice or stereotype—it's my impulse to try to level the playing field. You look for consistency? That, I think, is it.

In any case, despite my best efforts, Yusef Salaam was convicted. I think he was convicted on evidence that should never have been allowed into a courtroom.

KERRY. You honestly think he's innocent?

KUNSTLER. In his case, yes, I honestly do. And when you have every-one—and I'm not just talking about some shameless, self-aggrandizing thug trying to raise a lynch mob with a full-page ad in the *Times*, I'm talking about people who should know better—leaders in the black community—ministers even—all these people competing to see how quickly they can bury these guys, then I think you've got to respond firmly and publicly. Anyway, I do. I've got to. It is one of the true regrets of my career that I wasn't able to be of more use to Mr. Salaam. And I must tell you, my young friend, I regret that more than I do having fallen short in your eyes.

KERRY. But it's not just a matter of who you defend. *How* is impor-tant, too. The black guy who shot up the train on Long Island, the commuter train.

KUNSTLER. Colin—

KERRY. (Over.) Colin Ferguson gets onto the train, starts firing at everyone he can see. Twenty-five people shot, six killed. And what do you call it? "Black rage." Black rage? Your theory—he killed those people because he went nuts because of his experience with racism. That was the thrust of your—

KUNSTLER. I didn't claim that he didn't do it.

KERRY. But because of his experiences—being the victim of racism—this so unhinged him that he couldn't be held legally accountable.

KUNSTLER. I was going for an insanity defense. I mean, the guy *was* nuts. He ended up dumping me and my partner and defended himself.

KERRY. He was convicted.

KUNSTLER. Well, yes, of course he was.

KERRY. And you think—

KUNSTLER. I think he should be in a mental institution, not a jail.

KERRY. And your diagnosis was this black rage idea?

KUNSTLER. That was my belief.

KERRY. Do you think that being born black, just by virtue of that, you're entitled to rage?

KUNSTLER. I think it's understandable. Given the history of this country. I think it's understandable to be angry.

KERRY. You know I'm not arguing that. If we were talking about the riots after they shot Dr. King or after those cops were acquitted by a white jury out in LA—even though they'd been caught *on video*—if we were talking about crowds caught up in passion after those events, those provocations, then I could see you using that—But Colin Ferguson? To suggest that his unhinged violence merited the dignity of being deemed a justified defense. By that logic you could justify anyone black committing a crime. For instance, if I shot you, would you take my case?

KUNSTLER. If you shot me, I probably wouldn't be in any shape to take your case. But, you know, I probably *would* take your case.

KERRY. And what would be my defense? Mitigating circumstances?

KUNSTLER. Well, we'd have to delve into why you wanted to shoot me.

KERRY. OK, delve. Why would I want to shoot you? Because I'm a woman? Because I'm black? Because I'm a black woman and you're a big, old white guy who pushed the wrong buttons and I couldn't help myself? You have to see—this black rage idea—the implications. To expect different standards to apply because of skin color. That this could be used as a defense. It's another kind of racism. That you of all people could put an idea like that out there. Given who you were.

KUNSTLER. Were?

A beat, then Kerry lets loose.

KERRY. My father was in the movement. He was arrested in Mississippi. The removal statute got him out. *You* got him out. He told me about it. I'm sorry, but, yes I am disappointed. That story I grew up with, about what you did—You're one of the reasons I wanted to be a lawyer!

A beat.

KUNSTLER. Would you be happier if I died earlier? Before I had the chance to disappoint you?

A beat. She realizes she has gone too far.

KERRY. No, of course not.

A beat.

KUNSTLER. If I had something to do with you wanting to be a lawyer, that's something I'm proud of. I suspect you'll be a good one.

A beat. Outside, the demonstrators in the distance: "Kunstler must go."

KERRY. I don't want you to think I—

KUNSTLER. Hey, if anybody knows about getting carried away...

A beat.

KERRY. I hope you have a good birthday.

KUNSTLER. Thank you.

Kunstler nods and exits. The demonstrators fade away. A beat. Lights shift to a new setting supporting Kerry's epilogue.

KERRY. Shortly after this, Kunstler has heart surgery. Then, against the advice of his doctors, two days later William Kunstler insists on performing at his birthday party at Caroline's comedy club. Some believe that he overexerted himself that night. He dies a little over a month later.

The light on the podium goes out.

Nearly seven years later, in June 2002, a convicted murderer and rapist named Matias Reyes claims that he was responsible—he *alone*—for the attack on the Central Park jogger. His DNA is tested against DNA taken from the victim. It is a match. In view of this, the Manhattan District Attorney recommends that the conviction of Yusef Salaam and the four other defendants be overturned. And, on December 19, 2002, this happened. Yusef Salaam was released from prison. So, yes, it has to be said, William Kunstler was proven right about this, too.

> *The stage has grown dark except for a light on Kerry during the above passage. Suddenly, as we hear him, the lights come back up and Kunstler is there and vital across the house from her.*

KUNSTLER. No, no, no, no, no! You *still* don't understand: Whether he was guilty or not isn't the point! He deserved the best possible defense whatever he was!

> *Kerry is facing away from him during this.*

KERRY. God in heaven, Kunstler, you're dead. Even now can't you shut up?

> *A beat. Kunstler takes this in and smiles.*

Oh hell, you're going to hug me now, aren't you?

> *He opens his arms wide. Kerry finally turns to face him. The lights fade out.*

End of Play

AUTHOR'S NOTE

I blew my chance to have a real conversation with William Kunstler. Sometime in the 1980s, I found myself sitting with him and several others in a restaurant in Atlanta after the performance of a play I believe a friend of his had been involved with. I remember thinking in the moment that I was screwing up my opportunity to engage with an honest-to-God historical figure, but I was exhausted from a long day of running workshops, and I could barely say my name. An opportunity lost.

Flash forward to 2011. Watching a documentary called *William Kunstler: Disturbing the Universe*, it occurred to me that my friend Jeff McCarthy looked more than a little like the subject of the film. I called Jeff with this observation. He watched the film and called me back. "I could play this guy." I said that if he were interested, I'd look into writing a play.

The documentary was co-directed by two of Kunstler's daughters, Emily and Sarah. They made it, in part, as an apology to their departed father. They had disagreed with some of the cases he had chosen to take on late in his career, particularly his volunteering to represent Yusef Salaam, one of the young men accused in the Central Park jogger case. When Salaam was exonerated, some years after Kunstler's death, they felt the need to make public their acknowledgment that he had indeed been right. (They also apologized to Salaam.) Their disagreement was an echo of a number of others who, while sharing political sympathies with Kunstler in the '60s and '70s, had difficulties with aspects of his later career.

I have long been fascinated by public figures who undermine the reputations they built when they were young by choices in their final years. For a time, I kicked around writing a play about Marshal Pétain. Beloved in France as one of the heroes of World War I, he was branded a traitor when, in his eighties, he allowed himself to be used as the figurehead of the Vichy government during World War II. Of course, nothing Kunstler did was remotely as egregious as what Pétain did, but his reputation took a hit when he represented John Gotti and other notorious clients. The chance to explore someone who appeared to outlive his time appealed to me. (I hope the play makes a case for Kunstler not having done so.)

Kunstler's remarks in court are part of the public record so I was free to use them, but I wanted to be able to draw on his private thoughts, too. *My Life as a Radical Lawyer*, the memoir he wrote with the help of Sheila Isenberg, was a necessary source. To acquire the rights to draw from it, I had to make a deal with the family.

I contacted Emily and Sarah. They proposed that Jeff and I meet them at the Waverly Inn, a coffee shop in Greenwich Village. When we arrived, they informed us that their father had often consulted with clients in the very booth where we were seated. They looked at Jeff and said, yes, they could see him playing the part.

They wanted to know how I proposed going about the project. I told them that I was not interested in following the pattern of other plays about notable figures and writing a solo show. I told them I felt there had to be someone to challenge their father, just as they had sometimes challenged him in life. I think initially Emily and Sarah were wary that I might make them characters in the play, but I said I was thinking of structuring it as a seminar at a law school and that I saw the other character as a student who would confront him. (My friend Ralph Sevush told me of attending one of Kunstler's seminars and that some in the audience had indeed tried to give him grief.) This was how Kerry was born. Emily and Sarah agreed to let me use the material in the memoir if I followed that seminar construct. Beyond that, they asked for and received no right of approval regarding the content of the play.

I found *My Life as a Radical Lawyer* enormously useful in illuminating Kunstler's perspective, but very little of the language from the book found its way into the play. There is a substantial difference between what holds a page and what compels onstage. Much of the language in the book can't be spoken comfortably, something that is evident in the cassette recording of excerpts from it that Kunstler recorded. He sounds constrained by the text that is supposed to represent his voice. When I realized how little of that text was quotable for the play, it liberated me to try to create language that sounded plausible when spoken and also served the needs of drama. I have been pleased that none of the many people who have seen the play and knew Kunstler have challenged the accuracy of the voice I found.

Jeff McCarthy has frequently appeared at Barrington Stage in Pittsfield, Massachusetts, and he told its artistic director, Julianne

Boyd, of our project. She invited us to put up a reading of an early draft on September 3 and 4, 2011. She directed Jeff, with DeWanda Wise playing Kerry.

A reading featuring Jeff and Keona Welch was sponsored the following season by the Hudson Stage Company. It went well and Hudson Stage committed to producing it in the spring of 2013.

As it happened, Jeff was performing in a musical called *Southern Comfort*, co-starring Annette O'Toole. In 1972, Annette had been in a Los Angeles workshop of a very early musical I had written, but we had lost contact, though I had kept track of her subsequent accomplishments in TV and film. Jeff shared the script with Annette, who offered a smart observation that prompted me to revise the script. Jeff said that he had a hunch that Annette would make a good director for the project. I met with her, we resumed our friendship, and Hudson Stage agreed to engage her. The Hudson Stage production, featuring Jeff and Keona, did very well, both with the press and the audience.

One of the particular pleasures of the run was that people connected with Kunstler made the trek to Westchester to see the show. Members of Kunstler's family seemed to be pleased (and relieved). Kunstler's former law partner, Ron Kuby, also joined us and was enthusiastic. Particularly gratifying was the visit of Yusef Salaam, who also embraced the play. As luck would have it, I was not at the performance attended by both Salaam and Kuby, but a photo exists of Jeff and Keona posing with them, all four all smiles.

Jeff's friend Glenn Roven thought an audio production would work and Annette directed again, this time with Crystal Dickinson as Kerry. It is available through Audible.com.

In order to give the play further life, I decided to put up a barebones version in the New York Fringe. Kristine Niven, artistic co-director of AND Theatre Company (and also my wife) offered to help produce. Then Jeff got a gig playing Higgins in *My Fair Lady* at the Guthrie. Nick Wyman volunteered to take on the role despite the huge size of the part, the tinyness of the venue and the shortness of the run. Gillian Glasco joined us as Kerry. In the meantime, Annette had picked up a lead in a film to be shot when we were scheduled to rehearse, and I needed to find a director who would be willing to step in under the circumstances.

I had long admired Meagen Fay as a performer, both at Second City in Chicago and in stage and film roles. She had done a memorable turn in an Off-Broadway musical Melissa Manchester and I wrote, called *I Sent a Letter to My Love* (based on Bernice Rubens's novel). I knew that she had directed a few projects in Los Angeles. Though I had not seen them, I had the hunch she would do well with *Kunstler*. When I phoned to find out if she were interested, she asked me, "Is this because I knew him?" By utter coincidence, it turned out that her uncle, William Cunningham, was a Jesuit professor of law from Loyola University in Chicago and often consulted with Kunstler. Indeed, during the Chicago Seven trial, defendants Abbie Hoffman and Jerry Rubin often crashed at Meagen's home, and she has child-hood memories of sitting across the table from them at breakfast. Kunstler had been a frequent enough presence in her life for her to call him Uncle Bill. Her personal relationship with him couldn't help but inform the production.

The Fringe run was exhilarating. We sold out instantly (OK, the house only had fifty seats, but still...) and the show was warmly received by the press.

Then came a piece of luck. Patricia Snyder and her husband, William, invited me to bring a version of the Fringe production to Saratoga Springs. As it happened, Nick and Gillian were not free, so I asked Jeff if he were inclined. He was. I asked Nambi E. Kelley, an actor and playwright I much admired from her work in Chicago theatre, if she were game to play Kerry. She was. We pulled the piece together in the living room of Nambi's apartment and went to Saratoga to present three performances (January 30–February 1, 2015). Pat and Bill were so taken by its reception that they proposed that their company, the Creative Space International, bring the play to New York for an Off-Broadway run. (AND Theatre Company served as an associate producer.) We opened on February 17, 2017, in a space at 59E59 Theaters for a four-week run. Then, in an especially gratifying devel-opment, Julianne Boyd invited us back to Barrington Stage, playing a run that summer in the same space where the play had received its first reading. That proved so successful that we were asked to return for an encore run at the end of the summer. (Nambi was busy at Baltimore's Center Stage with the rehearsals of a play she had written, so we were joined for the Barrington engagement by Erin Roché.)

All of which is to say that this play has had the good fortune of being helped by many talented and committed people, and I am grateful to them all.

So much for the history of the project.

The play was written so that it can be satisfactorily produced with a minimum of resources. The New York Fringe version was so simply done that it took barely fifteen minutes to set up and break down the scenic, lighting, and audio elements. When offered larger budgets, the play has been done effectively in more elaborate environments. The Hudson Stage production was given in a design that invoked a wood-paneled Ivy League lecture hall; the 59E59 production was given in a more modern setting and included an effigy of Kunstler that was found by Kerry hanging from a lighting fixture as she entered the hall. (Both sets were designed by the resourceful James Fenton.) Both productions used lights and sound cues to shape the episodes, at times creating the illusion of pulling us into Kunstler's head.

A few thoughts that might be useful for interpretation:

When he arrives, Kunstler can sense Kerry's resistance to him, and he probably can guess much of the reason for it. (After all, as I've mentioned, his own daughters weren't shy about disagreeing with him.) His objective (aside from telling the stories he feels he has to share) is to win Kerry over. To this end, he constantly looks for opportunities to involve her in his presentation, and he keeps trying to get her to crack a smile.

Kerry is there out of a sense of duty. Her aim is to behave professionally and courteously and to maintain her poise. She puts a high premium on seriousness, which makes her a natural target for Kunstler's playfulness. She can't help but be moved by his apparent fragility, nor can she forget the mythic place he occupied in her household when she was growing up, but she has been disillusioned by some of his behavior during the last few years and isn't inclined to dismiss that. Also, it has to be acknowledged that, as charming as he thinks he is being, he is imposing his will on her and she is exercising restraint in not challenging him publicly.

Achieving adulthood is partially a matter of declaring independence from your parents and figures that have loomed large when you were young. In *Henry IV, Part 2*, Shakespeare has Hal metaphorically kill both his father and Falstaff; doing so is necessary to his growth.

Kerry isn't intentionally trying to kill Kunstler, but she does prompt him to say, "Would you be happier if I died earlier? Before I had the chance to disappoint you?" (I think this is the climax of the play.) She is shocked that he could so interpret her behavior, but there is a kernel of truth that she recognizes. Kunstler was one of the ones who paved the way so that both she and her father could make choices that were previously denied to them. But the passing of time will inevitably remove him and she will be among those who will have to step up. What she learns is that, even as she challenges aspects of his methods, she must both honor the past and learn from it.

And she also comes to realize that at times it doesn't hurt to be a little forgiving. After all, we're all human.

Except for Roy Cohn.

PROPERTY LIST

(Use this space to create props lists for your production)

SOUND EFFECTS
(Use this space to create sound effects lists for your production)

Note on Songs/Recordings, Images, or Other Production Design Elements

Be advised that Dramatists Play Service, Inc., neither holds the rights to nor grants permission to use any songs, recordings, images, or other design elements mentioned in the play. It is the responsibility of the producing theater/organization to obtain permission of the copyright owner(s) for any such use. Additional royalty fees may apply for the right to use copyrighted materials.

For any songs/recordings, images, or other design elements mentioned in the play, works in the public domain may be substituted. It is the producing theater/organization's responsibility to ensure the substituted work is indeed in the public domain. Dramatists Play Service, Inc., cannot advise as to whether or not a song/arrangement/recording, image, or other design element is in the public domain.

NOTES
(Use this space to make notes for your production)